PRIMARY READERS
PRE-STARTERS

Mole at the Seaside

Julie Davies
Illustrated by Estelle Corke

Richmond PUBLISHING

This is Mole.

He is at home, in the country.

Mole's eyes are very small.
He can't see! Mole is sad.

Seagull is at work. Look!
There are some glasses!

Mole has got glasses.
Thank you, Seagull!

"I can see!" says Mole.

Mole is very happy.
He can see the garden, the sunset...

Mole has got a book.
Thank you, Seagull!

Look! It's the seaside!

"A holiday!" says Mole.
"To the seaside!" says Seagull.

Mole is at the seaside. Seagull has got sunglasses and a camera for Mole! Thank you, Seagull!

Mole is on the beach with his
new friends Crab and Puffin.
It's hot!

What's this?

It's a sandcastle!
A beautiful sandcastle.

One, two, three, four, five, six, seven, eight, nine, ten, eleven, twelve,

thirteen, fourteen, fifteen, sixteen,

seventeen, eighteen, nineteen, twenty!

Ready!

Mole and his friends are at the funfair.
It's fun!

Mole is in a big tunnel!
He is happy!

Mole is at sea!

Mole is under the sea with the fish
and the seahorses.

He has got a beautiful pearl.

But, oh! Look!

Goodbye! Goodbye, seaside.
Goodbye, friends.

"Let's go home!" says Seagull.

Mole has got a good idea.

Hello! A holiday in the country!

Picture Dictionary

beach

camera

country

crab

fish

friends

funfair

garden

glasses

Picture Dictionary

holiday

mole

pearl

puffin

seagull

seahorse

seaside

sunset

tunnel